# SARAH DESSEN

LIBRARY
NASH COMMUNITY COLLEGE
P. O. BOX 7488

# SARAH DESSEN

GINA HAGLER

ROSEN PUBLISHING
New York

Published in 2014 by The Rosen Publishing Group, Inc.
29 East 21st Street, New York, NY 10010

Copyright © 2014 by The Rosen Publishing Group, Inc.

First Edition

All rights reserved. No part of this book may be reproduced in any form without permission in writing from the publisher, except by a reviewer.

**Library of Congress Cataloging-in-Publication Data**

Hagler, Gina.
Sarah Dessen/Gina Hagler.—First edition.
pages cm.—(All About the Author)
Includes bibliographical references and index.
ISBN 978-1-4777-1768-4 (library binding)
1. Dessen, Sarah—Juvenile literature. 2. Women authors, American—20th century—Biography—Juvenile literature.
I. Title.
PS3554.E8455Z65 2014
813'.54—dc23
[B]

2013013515

*Manufactured in the United States of America*

CPSIA Compliance Information: Batch #W14YA: For further information, contact Rosen Publishing, New York, New York, at 1-800-237-9932.

# CONTENTS


INTRODUCTION ............................6

CHAPTER ONE BIRTH TO COLLEGE............9

CHAPTER TWO BECOMING A NOVELIST............22

CHAPTER THREE A BEST SELLER....................35

CHAPTER FOUR MORE BOOKS FOLLOW...............48

CHAPTER FIVE BALANCING HOME AND WORK...........66

FACT SHEET ON SARAH DESSEN.........80

FACT SHEET ON SARAH DESSEN'S WORK................81

CRITICAL REVIEWS....................86

TIMELINE...........................93

GLOSSARY..........................95

FOR MORE INFORMATION.........97

FOR FURTHER READING.......101

BIBLIOGRAPHY...........104

INDEX.............109

# INTRODUCTION

Some kids pretend they are astronauts. Others pretend they are first responders. Some imagine themselves as teachers or lawyers, dancers or gymnasts, superheroes or secret agents. From her earliest memories, Sarah Dessen loved to write. By the time she was eight or nine years old, she was busy typing her stories on a manual typewriter at a desk in the corner of the family den. She couldn't know at the time that she would grow up to be a best-selling author for young adults. All she knew was that she loved to write.

Not everyone who loves to write becomes a successful author. The same is true for those aspiring to be astronauts, first responders, teachers, lawyers, dancers, gymnasts, superheroes, or secret agents. Becoming any of these requires a combination of talent, hard work, and a bit of luck. The path to a goal is not always a straight one. It's not unusual for people to encounter side roads and detours that may or may not lead to what they'd planned. Some give up at the first hint of trouble. Others persist and yet are unable to attain their goal. What they do when

Author Sarah Dessen has loved to write since she was a child.

they meet obstacles determines whether or not they are ultimately successful.

Dessen took a chance and pursued professional writing rather than other opportunities. Success came early in her career. Sustaining that success took more hard work and focus. She followed up her first successful novel with another, and then another that was equally successful. She accomplished this through determination and faith in her abilities.

It also took talent—especially the ability to create a world in each book that is real and engaging for her readers. Not everyone can write about first love or friendship in a way that will grip readers and compel them to tell their friends about the great book they are reading. It takes talent to bring everything together in a compelling story.

So how did Dessen do it? In the pages that follow, you'll read about the influences in her life, including her parents, her friends, and her experiences growing up. You'll see the role that persistence and belief in herself played in her success. You'll learn about her books and see the effort required to attain and sustain a career as a best-selling author.

The work involved in becoming an author is not for everyone. You need talent. You need determination. If you have enough of both, who knows what you can achieve?

CHAPTER

# BIRTH TO COLLEGE

Writers come from all types of childhood homes. Some writers emerge from home environments that would appear to stifle creativity. Others emerge from homes that seem to have been designed specifically to nurture a budding writer. Sarah Dessen came from a home that was closer to the second type—a home filled with books, stories, and parents who encouraged and supported their daughter's passion for all things words.

## CHILDHOOD

Sarah Dessen was born in Evanston, Illinois, on a summer day in 1970. The younger of two siblings, she had an older brother who loved music. In 1973, the family moved to Chapel Hill, North Carolina, where her parents took positions as professors at the University of North Carolina. Her mother, Cynthia Dessen, was a classicist. Her father, Alan Dessen, was an English professor. Given her parents'

Dessen's parents were professors at the University of North Carolina at Chapel Hill.

professions, it was inevitable that Dessen would grow up with literary influences. It's no surprise that from an early age, she was familiar with classic myths and the origins of words. She was also familiar with the works of William Shakespeare. Not a bad beginning for a future novelist!

She remembers reading from an early age and credits her love of reading to the fact that her parents were readers, too. However, it wasn't always fun being the child of literature professors. On her Web site, SarahDessen.com, she recalls, "I used to get frustrated with my mom because she bought me books for Christmas when what I really wanted were the gifts my friends got, things like sweaters and jewelry." Despite her initial disappointment, she continued to be an enthusiastic reader.

When she was in elementary school, Sarah Dessen typed her stories on a manual typewriter.

Dessen has been writing for as long as she can remember. When she was about nine, her parents gave her an old manual typewriter. They set up the typewriter at a desk in a corner of the den. It was here that Dessen wrote and typed her stories. She says that one result of her early interest in writing was her "tendency to embellish." She explains on her Web site, "I think it's just a weakness of fiction writers. Once you learn how to make a story better, it's hard not to do it all the time." Dessen's love of both reading and writing continued to grow as she made her way through middle school and went on to high school.

## HIGH SCHOOL

High school is often referred to as "the best years of your life." Dessen disagrees with this description, writing in her blog, "High school was NOT, in fact, the best time of my life." She told the *Pittsburgh Post-Gazette*, "You're not supposed to have it all figured out in high school. If you knew it all, and it was the best, it's all downhill from there."

Whether they're a high point or a low point, there is no doubt that the high school years are a time when there are a lot of changes in a person's life. Friendships come and go, and many important decisions must be made about the future. Those

## TEEN READER

Some of Sarah Dessen's favorite books from adolescence are ones she still clearly remembers today. The author says on her Web site, "The books I read when I was a teenager, the good ones anyway, have stuck more in my mind than anything since. I still love books, but while I couldn't tell you complete plots of novels I read even six months ago, I do remember even the smallest descriptive details from Lois Lowry's *A Summer to Die* or Judy Blume's *Are You There God? It's Me, Margaret.*"

These books struck her and stayed with her because in them she discovered authors who understood what she felt. They seemed to be speaking directly to her, and because of that, the messages in the books resonated with her. Dessen says, "I hope that my books do that for the people who read them...I think it's the best thing to which any writer can aspire."

changes and decisions make excellent material for novels. So do those first romantic relationships.

Dessen often creates her male characters using traits of the boys she was drawn to as a teen. The boys she liked are clearly remembered fondly. They are often funny, self-deprecating, and stand a bit on the outside of the main social group. "Girls always want to know: Are these boys real, and if so, where are they because I want to find them, " Dessen says in a 2011 video from Penguin Young Readers. Her warm memories have enabled her to create male characters that tend to be likeable.

Despite the fact that Dessen couldn't wait to get out of high school, her current best friend, Bianca, was a high school friend. Many of her other high school friendships also remain strong. In fact, Dessen still gets together with some of these friends for dinners and spa days. "We met when we were fifteen or so, and have seen each other through boyfriends, college, marriage, and now children and careers," she writes on her blog.

Another big part of her high school life—in fact, her entire life—has been basketball. In her hometown of Chapel Hill, where basketball is close to a "religion," the sport played a major role. She often blogs about basketball, and she posts UNC-related photos on Tumblr. A high point for Dessen was the time basketball legend Michael Jordan handed out candy at a friend's house on Halloween. She kept the Jolly Rancher he gave her for years.

Of course, high school is also a time for academic work and preparation for college. Dessen admits she was a bit of a "burnout" in high school. On her Web

The University of North Carolina Tar Heels basketball team plays for a sea of fans in Carolina blue and white. Basketball has always played a large role in Dessen's life.

site, she recalls that she spent a lot of time in the parking lot rather than in the classroom. Although she's short on the details, she shares that her senior quote was from the band Pink Floyd: "The time is gone, the song is over, thought I'd something more to say."

Dessen says, "It pretty much summed up my future, although I didn't know it at the time." Her highly successful young adult (YA) novels, which draw upon her wellspring of high school memories, make it clear she had a great deal to say.

In her senior yearbook, Dessen quoted lyrics from the Pink Floyd song "Time." The words proved to be prophetic.

## COLLEGE

Dessen's college years were not all smooth. After graduating from high school, Dessen entered Greensboro College to study advertising. It was a false start, and less than two months later she left the school, certain that advertising was not for her. She says on her blog, "So I think it all worked out. Aside from the whole dropping-out-of-school-the-first-semester-when-your-parents-look-on-with-shame thing."

She returned home and enrolled at the University of North Carolina at Chapel Hill to study creative writing. It was there that she took her first college writing course. The instructor was Doris Betts, a well-regarded southern writer and longtime creative writing professor. Dessen credits Betts with teaching her what she needed to become a successful novelist. She includes her professor in the acknowledgments for *That Summer*.

As an honors student at UNC, Dessen wrote her first novel, *The Daisy Chain*. She says on her blog, “It is, in a word, terrible. I think I eventually finished it...but I have no idea how it ended.”

While in college, Dessen met, dated, and lived with the man who is now her husband, Jay. During this time, she also worked as a waitress at the Flying Burrito restaurant. She credits her waitressing job with giving her ample opportunity to observe people and listen to their conversations, which gave her plenty of material to use as an author.

At the time, it was difficult for her to know which of her experiences would become important milestones or future sources of inspiration. Now it's clear to see that many of her experiences provided fodder for her novels while honing her “writer's ear” in the process.

In 1993, Dessen graduated from the University of North Carolina at Chapel Hill with highest honors in creative writing. She knew that she didn't want to head for a traditional career. She wanted to write novels. She had her senior thesis and the start of another novel. She eschewed what she refers to on her Web site as the "whole résumé/pantyhose thing," and decided to keep waitressing and make a serious attempt at achieving publication. At the time, she had no way of knowing if her efforts would be successful. She did know that for someone who had been a child with a wild imagination, her plan just might work.

CHAPTER

# BECOMING A NOVELIST

It's customary for young adults to begin a "real" job or head on to graduate school to pursue an advanced degree after college graduation. Sarah Dessen had other plans. She kept her job at the Flying Burrito and settled down in a little house to write a novel. It wasn't quite what her parents had in mind, but they were supportive as she tackled this task.

Writing a novel is not easy. There are many parts that must come together to create a whole. The dialogue, descriptions, motives, settings, and story all must meld and ring true to the reader. Perhaps most important, the writer must develop a "voice"—the personality behind the narration—that fits the story while attracting and holding the reader's attention. In

In addition to paying the bills, Dessen's job serving food at the Flying Burrito allowed her to observe people and develop an ear for dialogue.

Dessen's early writing, her voice began to emerge from the kind of stories she told.

## FINDING HER VOICE

Dessen actually worked on two novels immediately after graduation. The first she describes on her Web site as "marginally better" than her college thesis. The second was *That Summer*. Published three years after her graduation, the novel went on to be

Dessen's agent said that her voice was perfect for young adult literature.

wildly successful. It also established Dessen as a YA writer to watch.

She naturally gravitated toward a teenage narrator for *That Summer*. The book tells the story of fifteen-year-old Haven, who must deal with some complicated issues in her life. She is very tall for her age and finds it difficult to feel at ease with herself. Her father is remarrying after an illicit affair with a coworker. Her sister Ashley is marrying someone that Haven just doesn't see as husband material. Her relationship with her best friend is suddenly stormier than she'd like. Further, Haven is dealing with her feelings about her sister's ex-boyfriend—the one Haven wishes her sister were marrying.

Dessen says it was easy for her to connect with her own experiences as a teen when she was

## OTHER BEST-SELLING YA AUTHORS

Sarah Dessen is certainly not the only best-selling YA author. The following authors have also been successful in writing for those in their teens and early twenties:

- Suzanne Collins is best known for the *Hunger Games* trilogy. The books tell of a future world in which there is an annual contest to see who can escape alive. When Katniss Eberdeen volunteers to take her sister's place in the games, everything changes. *The Hunger Games* has been made into a movie.
- John Green is an author whose work has made the *New York Times* best-seller lists. His novel *The Fault in Our Stars* is based on his experiences working with children with life-threatening illnesses. *Looking for Alaska*, his first novel, received the Michael L. Printz Award from the American Library Association (ALA) in 2006.
- Stephenie Meyer is the author of the *Twilight* series. These highly successful books feature vampires, werewolves, and their relationships with humans, particularly the young Bella Swan. The series has been made into movies that have been huge box-office successes.
- J. K. Rowling burst onto the literary scene with her series about the boy wizard Harry Potter. Her books have been published in multiple languages

and were so popular that for the first time ever in children's book publishing, bookstores stayed open until midnight so that eager customers could purchase each new release. The books have been made into movies.

- Daniel Barnz's *Beastly* has been made into a movie of the same name. The novel and movie retell the story of *Beauty and the Beast*. This time it is set in present-day New York City.
- Sara Shepard's *Pretty Little Liars* book series led to a popular television series. Loosely based upon her life experiences, the series includes more than fifteen books.

Suzanne Collins, author of the *Hunger Games* trilogy, appeared at the 2012 premiere of the movie based on her work.

creating Haven's world. On her Web site, Dessen explains, "In high school I was lucky enough to have a big group of girlfriends that have really inspired a lot of the stories in my books. I'm still close with my friends from that time, so it's never very hard to put myself back into that place." She also continues to live in her hometown, which helps keep her high school memories—good and bad—fresh in her mind.

The author's own adolescence differed from that of the main character in her first published novel. Her own parents remained married, while Haven's were divorced. Yet Dessen's experiences as a daughter and her personal struggles with finding her place in the world added depth to her work.

Dessen had actually started writing with an adult audience in mind, but her literary agent, Leigh Feldman, suggested a teen audience would be a better fit. Dessen quickly realized that Feldman was right. She could see that her teenage narrator provided the perfect voice for a YA novel. Finding her voice allowed Dessen to clarify her vision for her future works. It also allowed her to picture herself as a writer who would touch the lives of teen readers in much the same way that her favorite authors had reached her as a teen. This was an important moment in her career.

## SOURCES OF INSPIRATION

Sources of inspiration are important for an author of fiction. Will the work be based on people, places, and things the author knows directly? Will it be based on research into a specific time or place? Depending on the type of novel that an author is writing, some research may be needed. In the case of a historical novel, the author needs to do enough research to pinpoint the details needed to bring the time alive for the reader. For an author like Sarah Dessen, who writes about contemporary life, much of the inspiration comes from personal experience.

As a YA author, it makes sense that Dessen draws inspiration from her high school experiences. She points out that living in her hometown keeps those memories, associations, and relationships alive. They are just beneath the surface of her current life, ready for her to use when she writes. She uses the people and places around her to create settings and situations that feel genuine and strike a chord with her readers. For example, the local mall plays a big part in *That Summer*.

In a video interview from Penguin Young Readers, Dessen says, "I often have a place, a concrete place in mind, that I know when I'm working." Having a place in mind helps her begin to create a

# SARAH DESSEN ON WRITING

In a 2011 video interview from Penguin Young Readers, Dessen uses Twitter to take questions from her fans. Readers ask such questions as what it takes to make a living as a writer and what one should do when faced with writer's block.

She says that making a living as a writer is not something that happens overnight. Even she, who had critical and fan support early in her career, worked as a waitress and teacher for nearly ten years before she could support herself with the proceeds from her books. She advises those who want to make a living as a writer not to expect to get rich quickly!

She also offers some useful advice about handling writer's block—the moments when a writer can't seem to get anything to work, or has no idea what to write next. Dessen believes that writer's block is an indication that you've gone off track somewhere in your writing. Maybe it's a new character that doesn't fit. Maybe it's a plot point that doesn't ring true. Her advice? Go back to the last place the writing was working and see what happened after that. She explains in the video, "When I get stuck, I go back to the last place that the writing was going well because usually it means that I did a wrong turn there. I added a character, I took a character away, I changed the setting—I did something that was a mistake." She says that going back and fixing the misstep can put you back on track.

Even for a writer as successful as Dessen, it took years for her to support herself solely from her writing.

setting. She then adds the elements she needs and subtracts those that play no part in the story she's telling.

The inspiration for Colby, the beach town in *Along for the Ride* and *What Happened to Goodbye*, is the town where Dessen spent her summers as a child. While Colby is not an exact model of that town, the flavor of the place, some of the businesses, and the proximity to the ocean are all true to life.

Growing up in a basketball-crazy town gave Dessen much of the background material for *What Happened to Goodbye*. She didn't have to stretch far to imagine the fervor that grips a university town before a big game. She also used her experience as a waitress at the Flying Burrito to capture life at a restaurant. In the video interview, she explains, "I always loved the chaos of the restaurant world. I think it's a great metaphor for just the chaos of life in general. That you have a lot of people thrown together, trying to accomplish a goal, which is honestly often just making it through the end of the night."

Dessen's family ties have also served as inspiration for the relationships in her writing. The author does not have a sister, but she does have an older

Dessen's older brother, Michael, watched shows like *Good Times* with her while they were growing up.

brother, Michael, who is a jazz musician. Dessen describes him as a very private person. Growing up, he taught her to drive a stick-shift car and was the person with whom she watched the television shows *Good Times* and *M*A*S*H*. She told *Horn*

*Book Magazine* that her brother was the "academic champion" in the family. She also has several cousins who have played an important role in her life.

Sources of inspiration can come from many places. They can come from study and research, stories told by others, or the actual experiences and emotional struggles of the author. Having a range of experiences gives an author a rich life. It also provides the material necessary for creating a world that rings true to readers.

With her voice and sources of inspiration firmly established, it wasn't long before Dessen had the first of many best-selling YA novels.

CHAPTER

# A BEST SELLER

Novelists like Sarah Dessen can appear to be overnight successes. It may seem as if they sit down, write a novel, send it out, and off they go. This is not true. Dessen's first published novel, *That Summer*, was actually the third novel she authored. She also paid her dues by majoring in creative writing in college and writing as a hobby all her life. She perfected her craft as a first step in achieving her success. If she hadn't, it's unlikely that her first novel would have become a best seller. It's also unlikely that her second novel, *Someone Like You*, would have been published at all, or that those first two books would have been made into the movie *How to Deal* from New Line Cinema. However, that

The setting of the local mall plays a large part in *That Summer*.

doesn't mean that every step in Dessen's career was as successful as the one before.

## THAT SUMMER

*That Summer* introduced the town of Lakeview, which is based on Chapel Hill, North Carolina, Dessen's hometown. The author told Sue Corbett of *Publishers Weekly*, "I put things in every book, these little overlaps of places and people thinking no reader will ever find them, and they're on the Internet immediately after the book is published." Readers were quick to spot the real-life versions of the Lakeview Mall and Milton's Market.

The reaction to *That Summer*, released in October 1996, was one that every first-time novelist dreams about: the book was well received. It sold very well. Book reviewers gave it high marks. A starred review in *Publishers Weekly* said, "First-time author Dessen adds a fresh twist to a traditional sister-of-the-bride story with her keenly observant narrative full of witty ironies.

Haven's struggles to feel comfortable with herself in *That Summer* rang true for many teen readers.

Her combination of unforgettable characters and unexpected events generates hilarity as well as warmth." *Kirkus Reviews* said that the book had an "appealing cast and droll humor."

The situations and characters were ones that a YA audience could relate to. With high school being a time of insecurity—with many teens feeling that they are too tall, too short, too fat, or too thin—Haven's struggles to feel comfortable in her 5-foot-11 (196 cm) frame made her instantly recognizable. Combine those struggles with one too many life changes and Dessen had created a teen-age protagonist that rang true. When Haven reexamined what she believed was a simpler and better time in her life, only to discover it wasn't at all what she thought, teen girls loved it.

## SOMEONE LIKE YOU

Dessen's second novel, *Someone Like You*, was released soon afterward, in 1998. Although fans were enthusiastic, the reception to the second book lacked the excitement of the first. However, the book sold well, and Dessen's reputation as a YA author of note was not diminished.

# SARAH DESSEN ON *THAT SUMMER*

*That Summer* was the first novel that Sarah Dessen sold. She wasn't famous. There were no expectations of what she would write. Without those expectations, Dessen says she wrote from the heart about a fifteen-year-old girl named Haven who was trying to get comfortable in her own skin. Her parents had gotten divorced. Her older sister was getting married to someone she wasn't wild about. She was too tall for her age. It all added up to one tumultuous time. To top it all off, Haven comes into contact with her sister's former boyfriend, Sumner Lee. He's the one Haven would have her sister marry.

Dessen says on her Web site, "When I look back over *That Summer* now, I always think that I was writing a bit more freely then because it was before I knew to worry about reviews or publishers or what everyone else thought. Sumner Lee, Ashley's long-lost boyfriend, has remained one of my very favorite characters of all time. Plus when I was planning my own wedding, I found that I could relate, in a way I never had before, to Ashley's Bad Bride Behavior (although I didn't always want to admit it)." Her husband's all-time favorite scene is a part of *That Summer*, too. It's the one in which Sumner films a cheese commercial.

*Someone Like You* is the story of Halley, a teen with a best friend, Scarlett, who is pregnant, and a new boyfriend, Macon, whom her parents forbid her to see. Halley just wants to be her own person. She pulls away from her mother and puts even more trust in Scarlett. *Publisher's Weekly* said in a May 4, 1998, review, "This romance/coming-of-age story is not as tightly written as Dessen's debut, *That Summer*...but Dessen's fully developed characterizations of charismatic teens, particularly the rebel-without-a-cause type Macon, are sure to attract readers—especially those who, like Halley, have felt the urge to take a walk on the wild side."

On her Web site, Dessen says that while *Someone Like You* is the book with the "biggest legion of fans," it is also the book that got the worst review. Unfortunately, that review came from the campus newspaper at her alma mater, the University of North Carolina. Worse, she was teaching in the university's writing program at the time. Dessen still remembers the challenge of walking into her classes after the paper awarded her book a zero out of five stars. She recalls, "It didn't matter that I'd gotten a decent review in the *New York Times* book section that same week: I carried around that bad *Daily Tar Heel* review for weeks, until one of my friends got sick of me looking at it and flushed it down the toilet."

## HOW TO DEAL

The mixed reviews for *Someone Like You* did not quash New Line Cinema's enthusiasm for a movie based on Dessen's work. According to IMDb.com, *How to Deal* was released on July 18, 2003. The movie was directed by Claire Kilner and had a screenplay by Neena Beber. *How to Deal* is based on two Dessen novels, *That Summer* and *Someone Like You*. It takes elements from each, changing some details and rearranging the timelines, to create one film containing all the major events. The movie stars Mandy Moore as Halley Martin and Alexandra Holden as Scarlett Smith, Halley's best friend.

Mandy Moore *(right)* and Alexandra Holden starred in the film *How to Deal*, which was based on Dessen's first two novels.

In *How to Deal*, Halley grapples with her father's remarriage, her mother's life after divorce, and her sister's upcoming wedding. She also deals with Scarlett's pregnancy, the death of Scarlett's boyfriend, and her feelings for Macon. Macon is definitely not the boy Halley's mother would want her to date, but at this point in Halley's life, her mother's wishes are the last thing she's interested in. The movie ends with the birth of Scarlett's baby as Halley and Macon reestablish their relationship.

The movie earned mixed reviews from critics. Peter Travers of *Rolling Stone* wrote, "The pop diva [Moore] goes down with the bubbles in this hopelessly shallow

Cast members Mandy Moore, Allison Janney, and Trent Ford attend the premiere of *How to Deal* in 2003. The movie was most popular with teenage girls.

soap opera." Richard Roeper wrote a more positive review: "I've seen a lot of dumb teen romances in the last couple of years, but *How to Deal* is a welcome exception."

Audiences were more appreciative. According to IMDb.com, *How to Deal* grossed nearly $6 million its opening weekend. The estimated budget for the movie was $16 million. Predictably, the movie was most popular with girls under the age of eighteen. One fan from Sydney, Australia, summed it up this way on IMDb.com: "I don't think it would win any awards, but it served its purpose well—it entertained me for a couple of hours—isn't that all we ask of a movie?"

## MOVING ON

So what did Dessen do when faced with some less-than-favorable reviews of her second book? After the *Daily Tar Heel* review was flushed, she sat down and wrote a third novel—and then a fourth and a fifth. In short, she kept writing. She had faith in her abilities and plenty of fan support. She continued teaching and writing, filling in more details about the town of Lakeview that figures so prominently in her books.

She actually has a special place in her heart for *Someone Like You*. "*Someone Like You* is special to me," she says on her Web site, "because it's dedicated to my best friend from high school, Bianca, who was there firsthand for all the real truths of us trying to survive high school, and knows even the stories I don't tell."

Her tenacity paid off. By May 2009, Dessen would have combined sales for her books of nearly four million copies, according to an article by Shannon Maughan in *Publishers Weekly*. Maughan wrote, "For many teen girls, it just wouldn't be summer without a new Sarah Dessen novel to kick back with."

CHAPTER

# MORE BOOKS FOLLOW

Sarah Dessen has been described as a perennial favorite with teenage girls. NPR.com included four of her books—*Just Listen, The Truth About Forever, Along for the Ride*, and *This Lullaby*—on its "100 Best-Ever Teen Novels List," published online in 2012. Her books are consistently on best-seller lists, and her fans anxiously await each new must-have romance.

Dessen's books are often set during the summer, which provides a contained time for the action to occur. The settings and characters often overlap with those in her other books. "Some of my favorite things about Sarah Dessen's novels are the connections she makes between her books," says blogger Heidi from *YA Bibliophile*.

"The places and people reappear in small scenes. It's so fun for me when I recognize something!"

The issues that Dessen's characters face are ones that are familiar to many teens. That's part of what gives her work its YA appeal. Even when an issue may not be part of a teen's personal experience, the way Dessen includes it in her character's story makes the issue real and compelling. "Dessen also has a knack for locating her stories in the exact, most heartrending crux of a character's struggle. The moment just before something big, something life-altering happens," says blogger Shannon Rigney Keane of the Girls Leadership Institute.

In the eleven books she's written to date, her characters have dealt with abandonment, divorce, eating disorders, and teen pregnancy. Here's a look at the way these thematic issues appear in individual books as well as across her body of work.

## ABANDONMENT

Abandonment plays a role in a number of Dessen's books. In many cases, such as in *Along for the Ride*, her work explores the emotional abandonment that takes place after divorce. In *Lock and Key*, the abandonment is literal and takes place when her mother's multiple addictions leave seventeen-year-old Ruby Cooper on her own. Ruby is forced to move in with

The issues in Dessen's books, such as divorce and abandonment, are ones her young adult readers can relate to.

her sister, which she finds difficult. The hardest part for Ruby is learning to trust people and let them get close enough to help her. She must also learn to accept and value her family as it is, although it is never going to be the one she might wish for.

## DIVORCE

Divorce plays a role in several of Dessen's novels. In *Along for the Ride*, Auden stays awake at night—a reaction to her parents' pre-divorce habit of arguing after she went to bed. Now her father is remarried and starting a new family, and Auden is not quite sure where that leaves her. When she's invited to spend the summer with her father, she resists before deciding it might just

In *What Happened to Goodbye*, the main character, Mclean, struggles to define herself when she moves to a new place.

be an adventure. As she spends time with her stepmother, Auden is forced to see her father in a new light. She's surprised by what she learns about his new wife. She also learns a lot about herself as she relates to her new baby sister. Once Auden is able to see her parents in a new way, she is able to move forward in her life.

*What Happened to Goodbye* also features divorce as a key element. Mclean's mother has remarried after an affair. As a result of that affair, she has new twins, a new husband, and a more upscale life. Mclean is furious with her mother and chooses to live with her father, a restaurant fixer who is always on the move. Each time she moves, Mclean tries on a new identity. She is the peppy girl at one school, and a quiet and studious girl at another. It all works until she has to be herself and realizes she's not really sure who that is anymore. The effects of her parents' divorce provide a realistic, steady drumbeat throughout the story.

In both books, the characters go about their lives with divorce as just one part of their lives, not one that necessarily defines them. Since the circumstances of the divorce are different in each case, the part that divorce plays in each story also differs. As a result, two books present two different views of teen life after divorce.

## DATING VIOLENCE

Relationship violence plays a huge role in the book *Dreamland*. Caitlin O'Koren is turning sixteen when her eighteen-year-old sister runs away on Caitlin's birthday. Her birthday forgotten, Caitlin feels personally overlooked and at the same time feels pressure to fill the role of her super-successful sister. It's too much for her, and she begins seeing a boy named Rogerson Biscoe. Everything is fine until Rogerson encourages her to use drugs. Her grades plummet, and her life begins to spiral out of control.

In a realistic portrayal of violence in teen relationships, Rogerson then begins to isolate Caitlin, making it nearly impossible for her to maintain relationships with her other friends. Not long after that, Rogerson begins to physically abuse Caitlin when she doesn't tell him each detail of her day. Things reach a boiling point when an incident occurs and Caitlin's mother becomes involved. Dessen tackles the difficult issue of relationship violence by focusing on Caitlin and her growing self-awareness.

## FRIENDSHIP

Friendships are key in all of Dessen's books. From the healthy friendships of *Along for the Ride* to the more dubious friendships of *Dreamland*, her realistic portraits of teen friendships help explain the enduring hold that her novels have on fans. The ups and downs of friendship during high school summers play a major part in her novels.

In *Someone Like You*, Halley and Scarlett have been best friends for years. Their friendship is a fairly typical one until the day Scarlett needs Halley's support with a serious problem. It's not a role Halley has played before, but she's eager to step up now that her friend needs her. In *Along for the Ride*, Auden is a girl who has always been on the outside. Her focus has been on schoolwork and little more. When she arrives at the beach town where she'll spend her summer, she knows nothing about the way girls relate. Her clumsy first steps are a bit painful for the reader, but by the end of the summer, she's more than confident in her ability to interact socially.

Mclean has more friends than she can count in *What Happened to Goodbye*. The problem is, none of them really know her. She's moved and changed her identity so often that she's not quite

Friendships are an important element in Dessen's novels.

sure when and how to reveal her true self. This dilemma—judging when a friend can be trusted with the most vulnerable parts of who you are—is one that teen readers can easily relate to. The author's sensitive treatment of Mclean's confusion, as well as the realistic reactions of Mclean's new friends when they discover the truth underneath the façade, makes this story of friendship ring true.

## GRIEVING

*The Truth About Forever* is the story of Macy and her grief over the sudden death of her father. It realistically portrays the confusion and missed opportunities for connection between family members that occur

# SARAH DESSEN ON HER BOOKS AS CULTURAL STUDIES

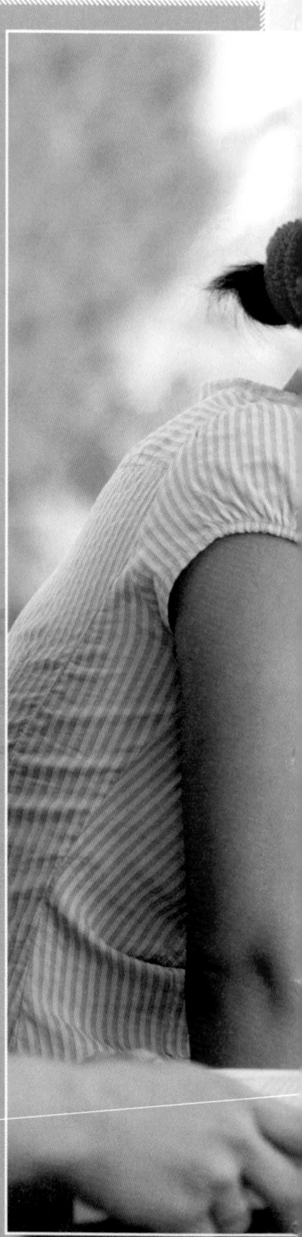

In a 2006 interview, Sue Corbett of *Publishers Weekly* asked Dessen if she thought of her books as cultural studies—materials that could be used one hundred years from now to see what life had been like for suburban American teens of this time.

Dessen replied that her books were not cultural studies so much as a peek inside adolescence, which is a universal experience. She told Corbett, "You remember that time of your life so vividly because there are so many firsts. You're learning your way." The letters she receives from her readers often say that her books accurately mirror their lives as teens.

It's made Dessen realize that even if some cultural factors change over the years, the core of the high school experience remains the same: "There's still the guy you're madly in love with who doesn't even know your name, and the friend who is intensely appealing even though she treats you like garbage. High school was like that before I was there and will be ages from now."

Dessen's books bring the core experiences of high school to life.

when a family is in grief. Macy's struggles to create a life without her father are also complicated by the fact that running with her father has been an important part of her life. For reasons that are integral to the story, she gives up running after his death. To make matters worse, her boyfriend says he needs a break at about the same time.

Dessen also explores death, grief, and what is enduring in life in *Someone Like You*. In this book, Scarlett's boyfriend is killed in a motorcycle accident shortly after the two express their love for one another. Meanwhile, Halley, Scarlett's best friend, is excited about the boy she's just getting to know. Halley doesn't always know how much she should share with Scarlett about her new relationship while she is grieving.

In *Along for the Ride*, several boys are close friends of Abe, who dies as the summer begins. Most of the boys deal with their grief by avoiding the topic, but the character Eli grieves by avoiding all of his friends. Instead, he wanders the town at night, unable to sleep.

While the specifics of their grief may differ, all of Dessen's characters come to realize that moving on after a death is more complicated than they expected. The depth of feeling in the books provides a thought-provoking and gripping way for readers to step into an experience that may not be familiar to them.

## HIGH SCHOOL ANGST

What YA reader can't relate to high school angst? From Ron trying to make sense of his feelings for Hermione in the Harry Potter books to Bella Swan of *Twilight* on those first uncomfortable days in a new school, high school angst is a familiar theme in young adult literature. It's no different for the characters in Dessen's novels. With characters like Auden in *Along for the Ride*, who has never had a group of close friends, and Scarlett in *Someone Like You*, who must deal with her entire high school learning she is pregnant, there's more than enough angst to go around. Even Annabel Green, the "It" girl in *Just Listen*, has her share of teen anxieties.

Dessen deals with all the turmoil of the high school years with a gentle touch. Her characters deal with their ups and downs in ways that ring true to the reader. There is no one way to get through high school successfully, and Dessen doesn't leave her readers with cookie-cutter answers. The uncertainty that each character experiences is part of the attraction for Dessen's growing legion of fans.

## RELATIONSHIPS

Relationships play vital roles in all of Dessen's books. There are relationships between parents,

Dessen's novels have plenty of boy-meets-girl romance.

daughters and mothers, daughters and fathers, boyfriends and girlfriends, and just plain friends. Each relationship is defined in a way that makes it more than a plot device. In *Along for the Ride*, Auden's relationship with her father is shaky at first, but ultimately it's strengthened by her ability to see her father as more than just her dad. The same is true for her relationship with her mother.

*This Lullaby* follows Remy Starr's attempts to form relationships while growing up with a mother who is on husband number five. Her brother is engaged, but as her mother's newest husband begins to cheat on her, Remy can't help but wonder if true love really exists. For readers who have divorced parents of their own, it's a safe way to explore ideas about love through a character they can relate to.

Dessen's work doesn't neglect plain old boy-meets-girl romance. There is more than enough in each of her books to ensure that her fans eagerly await each summer release. From insomniac love in *Along for the Ride* to abusive love in *Dreamland* and puppy love in *That Summer*, her readers are eager to see what comes next for her characters. The romances are not formulaic. Each romance has its own nuances and rhythm, in keeping with the characters that Dessen has created.

## SELF-ESTEEM

Self-esteem is a tricky concept. Some say that true self-esteem means knowing who you are and liking yourself anyway. Others say that self-esteem is a lifelong quest. In *Keeping the Moon*, Colie Sparks has always been chubby. Much like Mclean in *Along for the Ride*, she hasn't had many friends. However, in Colie's case, keeping her distance has been a strategy to protect herself from teasing. Now she's lost a lot of weight and is meeting people who never knew her as her former chubby self. That is confusing enough, but then the bully from her overweight days is back in her life. Colie is challenged to defend herself and maintain her newfound confidence or crawl back into a place of fear that is not right for who she has become. Any teens who have been bullied can understand why the bully has such a strong hold over Colie and her feelings about herself. They can also understand why it's so difficult for her to stand up for herself. Dessen's sensitive portrayal of Colie and her dilemma even grips readers who haven't experienced bullying firsthand.

CHAPTER FIVE

# BALANCING HOME AND WORK

Sarah Dessen published eleven books in the course of seventeen years. During those years, she got married, had a baby, and supervised the construction of a new home. She's visited schools, spoken at conferences, given interviews, and made videos about her books. She's had a very busy life, both personally and professionally. So how does she balance her home and work lives?

## BECOMING A MOM

Dessen married her college boyfriend, Jay Earl Marks, on June 10, 2000. By the time her daughter, Sasha Clementine, was born on Labor Day weekend in 2007, Dessen had seven books in print. Her eighth book, written and edited during her pregnancy,

Becoming a mother meant changing the way Dessen approached her writing.

was *Lock and Key*. It was released soon after her daughter's birth. In fact, one of the earliest photos of Sasha that Dessen posted online shows her in her infant seat, holding a copy of *Lock and Key*.

Her next book, *Along for the Ride*, was released just a year later. "A lot of people were surprised when it was announced that I'd have a new book coming out in summer 2009, only a year after my last novel, *Lock and Key*," says Dessen on her Web site. "I can relate. It was kind of a shock to me as well."

She explains that the combination of sleep deprivation and caring for a newborn gave her a new look at another side of life—the middle of the night. "I'd look out my window at three or four AM...see a light on in the distance, and wonder who else was up, and why. There was this whole other world at night, one I'd been completely unaware of, and it made me start thinking about the people who chose to live in it, and how they found themselves there. That's where Auden's story began."

Dessen wrote *Along for the Ride* in stolen moments while caring for her daughter. On her Web site, she says she worked on the book as a bit of an escape during this exciting but intense period. She wrote some parts while her daughter was sleeping and other parts while a babysitter was there. As a result, she wrote the book in a totally different way than usual, one that fit that time in her life. She explains, "It was a crazy and chaotic way to write a book, and not at all the kind of structured, methodical approach I'd always used before. And you know what? Somehow it just worked."

The key to Dessen's success after entering motherhood was her willingness and ability to be flexible. She tried new ways of organizing her time. She took advantage of any available chunks of time to add more to what she'd been writing.

"If there's one thing I've learned by having a kid," Dessen blogged in March 2010, "it's how to be present." What does that mean? It means staying in the moment and addressing what needs to be taken care of right now. With a young child in the equation, it became more difficult for her to plan and follow through exactly on those plans.

In her blog post, she explained that with a toddler, "forward thinking just doesn't work. She doesn't understand 'later' or 'sometime soon.' It's either happening now, or it isn't. And if it isn't, that's usually a reason to insist that it does, usually by screaming or stomping feet, whether that happening is reading another book or having a cookie." Focusing on the present was a new way of looking at life, but one that came with motherhood.

By the time *Along for the Ride* was published, Dessen had experience as both a published author and writing with a young child in the house. As she continued her writing career, she took time to be active in family events and in Sasha's life. She became involved in her daughter's preschool, planned birthday parties and tea parties, and rearranged her work schedule to include her new role as mother. For example, her school visits have become less frequent, but she still travels to conferences from time to time. She also tours to promote her books. Each trip is designed to use her time efficiently so that she can return home as soon as possible. In this way, she tries to meet the needs of both her daughter and her readers.

One way that Dessen is able to stay in touch with readers while being at home with her daughter is by blogging. Posts called "The Friday Five!" appear on her blog regularly, filling readers in on any news. Some posts are about motherhood, some are about her latest book, and others are just comments on what has happened in her life that week. For example, in one amusing post, she described her reaction to the chickens that her husband, Jay, bought for their family. She also shared news about the death of her dog and about the new dog that joined the family. Whatever the content, the message is clear: Dessen wants her readers to know that she values her connection with them and wants it to continue.

In her blog, Dessen often writes about the ways in which her family and book worlds merge—or collide. In a July 2011 post, she wrote about a book signing at which her family turned out to show their support. Her father was there, along with her nephew and daughter. Her father and nephew were excited to be part of the event. Her daughter? She was more interested in the arcade and toy store down the street.

## WORK DEVELOPMENTS

Dessen's latest book, *The Moon and More*, was released in June 2013. The main character, Emaline, spends the summer before college working for her parents' summer rental business in the beach town of Colby—a town that appears in several other Dessen novels. Dessen came upon the idea for the book while on a family vacation.

"Each time, I think I'm never going to write another book. It never gets easier," Dessen told an audience of fans at the Carnegie Library of Pittsburgh, according to *Publishers Weekly*. "After *What Happened to Goodbye*, we went [on a vacation] to the beach and I was reading by the pool. This young, shirtless pool guy comes out and we have a big old conversation. He was so chatty and funny, and sweet and cute. I thought, there's

Dessen enjoys interacting with her fans at book signings and other events.

my next book: what is it like to be permanent in a town where everything is temporary?"

Dessen also enjoys participating in social media. During a question-and-answer session at the library, she said, "Social media can suck up a lot of my time," and she admitted to a weakness for Pinterest and Twitter. She emphasized the importance of having a presence online for her readers, which she does in a variety of ways, including blogging and posting on social networking sites. "If you're writing for teens, you have to meet them on their turf," she said.

In addition to being flexible in her work habits, focusing on her writing when she can, and maintaining a presence on the Internet, Dessen also makes time for speaking engagements. With the

# KEEPING IN TOUCH WITH READERS

Communicating with her readers is a top priority for Sarah Dessen. She was one of the first YA authors to have a blog for her readers. To further facilitate communication, Dessen has her own social networking site called Sarah-land, hosted on Ning. The site includes a Twitter feed with live tweets about Dessen, another feed with her blog posts, and photos and videos. There's also a forum for members, as well as places for members to post their own content. There are more than twelve thousand members in this community of fans.

Dessen also posts on Twitter, Facebook, Tumblr, and Pinterest. Her tag on Pinterest describes her as "Author. Mother. Worrier." The content on her boards ranges from puppies to sources of inspiration. On Tumblr she posts a variety of pictures and clips. As for Twitter, Dessen tweets to nearly 213,000 followers each day. So far she has nearly twenty thousand tweets.

The author says she wishes there were enough hours in each day to write her books *and* reply to each fan personally. Because there isn't, using social media to maintain contact with her fans is very important to her.

launch of each new book, she appears at local events and goes on a larger national tour. For example, in 2013, she did a book tour for the paperback edition of *What Happened to Goodbye* and another tour in conjunction with the release of *The Moon and More*.

## LOYAL FANS

Dessen's devotion to her fans is returned by her fans' devotion to her. In addition to the posts that fans leave on Dessen's Sarah-land Web site, there are hundreds of fan-made book trailers, book reviews, and videos posted on YouTube. The book recommendations site Goodreads.com has fan groups for Dessen and for some of the characters in her novels. It also features more than fifty pages of memorable quotes from her novels, some with over twenty thousand "likes." Fans post trivia questions, too. In fact, for some books, readers can take an online quiz.

Dessen's fans also blog about her books on their personal blogs. Blog posts include reviews and detailed plot summaries of her books. WordPress.com alone hosts hundreds of blogs that are dedicated solely to Dessen or include posts about her books.

Her fans interact with one another through their comments on these sites. They also tweet about her with the hashtag #sarahdessen or hashtags with the names of characters in her books. These tweets often form a conversation among people who have never met. For her part, Dessen takes the

Dessen maintains an active online presence as a way of staying in touch with her readers.

time to make "blog tours"—appearances on a number of different blogs—when her new books are released. Fans post comments on these sites as well. All of this makes her more accessible to her fans.

Why are readers so committed to Dessen? Perhaps it is because she genuinely cares about her readers. When one man wanted to propose to his fiancée, who was a huge fan, Dessen helped him out by surprising her in New York. When another young woman asked the author to sign her book and Dessen misspelled her name, she didn't just fix it. She went to the register with her fan and bought her a brand-new book. Readers learn of these events through their posts. More readers leave comments or post about the posts. The result is a community of dedicated Dessen followers, waiting anxiously for each new release.

Speculation and anticipation before each new release also engage Dessen's fans. They create forums to guess at the new cover image. They eagerly search the Web for any hints about the content or release date of the next novel. Fans have learned that her novels are often released at the start of summer. This leaves teens plenty of time to read

Dessen's life as a writer suits her perfectly.

the newest work without the interruption of homework. It also gives them a terrific way to kick off their summer vacations.

## WRITING ON

In the biography on her Web site, Sarah Dessen describes her daily life, which includes many nonwriting activities involving her husband, child, dogs, and garden. She says she is partial to Starbucks mochas, even though they make her hyper. She boasts of making a mean bean salad and admits to having a life that is far less interesting than her books.

Dessen describes her career as a YA author as something that she never really intended. "Even though it was in a way accidental," she says, "I've found that writing for teens suits me. I do short stories, and other novels, that are for an older audience, but again and again I am brought back to the stories of high school."

About her writing, Dessen says, "I've found in my own life that if my writing isn't going well, not much else will. It's the one constant, the key to everything else. Now that I'm writing full-time, I have my good days and bad days. But I'd rather be doing this, even on the worst days, than anything else."

# FACT SHEET ON SARAH DESSEN

**Birth Date:** June 6, 1970

**Birthplace:** Evanston, Illinois

**Parents:** Alan and Cynthia Dessen

**Siblings:** One brother, Michael Dessen

**Hometown:** Chapel Hill, North Carolina

**First Publication:** *That Summer*, 1996

**Marital Status:** Married Jay Earl Marks on June 10, 2000

**Children:** One daughter, Sasha Clementine

**Colleges Attended:** University of North Carolina at Chapel Hill, Greensboro College

**Hobby:** Gardening

**Blog:** SarahDessen.com/blog

**Web Site:** SarahDessen.com

**Ning:** Sarah-land

**Twitter:** @SarahDessen

**Tumblr:** authorsarahdessen

**Pinterest:** DessenSarah

**Weaknesses:** Luke Perry, potato chips, infants, chocolate chip cookies, and anything Kate Spade

**Quote from Sarah Dessen:** "My setup, usually, is a character feeling disjointed and out of place…It's a pretty universal experience: much of adolescence is just trying to figure out where you fit in, where your spot is, who your people are."

# ON SARAH DESSEN'S WORK

*That Summer.* New York, NY: Orchard Books, 1996.

**Released:** October 1, 1996

**Summary:** Fifteen-year-old Haven must come to terms with the new reality of her life, letting go of her illusion of a perfect past in the process.

**Awards and Honors:** ALA Best Books for Young Adults (1997)

*Someone Like You*. New York, NY: Viking, 1998.

**Released:** May 1, 1998

**Summary:** Halley and Scarlett have been friends forever when the unexpected death of Scarlett's boyfriend leaves her needing Halley more than ever.

**Awards and Honors:** ALA Quick Pick, South Carolina Young Adult Book Award (2000–2001), *School Library Journal* Best Books of the Year

*Keeping the Moon*. New York, NY: Viking, 1999.

**Released:** September 1, 1999

**Editor:** S. November

**Summary:** Fifteen-year-old Colie has always been overweight. Now she's lost weight, and everything has changed.

**Awards and Honors:** ALA Quick Pick, New York Public Library's Book for the Teen Age (2000), *School Library Journal* Best Books of the Year

*Dreamland: A Novel.* New York, NY: Viking, 2000.

**Released:** September 1, 2000

**Editor:** Deborah Brodie

**Summary:** What do you do when your older sister runs away on your sixteenth birthday and you discover she's always envied you?

**Awards and Honors:** ALA Best Books for Young Adults (2001), New York Public Library's Books for the Teen Age (2001), ALA Popular Paperbacks for Young Adults (2003)

*This Lullaby.* New York, NY: Viking, 2002.

**Released:** May 27, 2002

**Summary:** Eighteen-year-old Remy has never believed in true love. How can she be sure that she has it with Dexter?

**Awards and Honors:** ALA Best Books for Young Adults (2003), New York Public Library's Books for the Teen Age (2003)

*The Truth About Forever.* New York, NY: Viking, 2004.

**Released:** May 11, 2004

**Summary:** Everything changes when Macy's father dies suddenly. How can all the pieces ever fit together?

**Awards and Honors:** ALA Teens' Top Ten (2005), ALA Popular Paperbacks for Young Adults (2011)

*Just Listen.* New York, NY: Viking Children's Books, 2006.

**Released:** April 16, 2006

**First Printing:** 100,000 copies

**Summary:** Annabel has never been as together as it seems. She's also not very good at speaking the truth. Then she meets Owen.

**Sales:** The book appeared on the *New York Times* children's chapter books best-seller list.

**Awards and Honors:** ALA Best Books for Young Adults (2007), ALA Teens' Top 10 (2007)

*Lock and Key.* New York, NY: Viking, 2008.

**Released:** April 22, 2008

**Summary:** Ruby Cooper has never had a family she could depend on. Then she is forced to move in with her sister and realizes that it's all in how you define family.

**Sales:** The book hit number one on the *New York Times* children's chapter books best-seller list.

**Awards and Honors:** ALA Amazing Audiobooks for Young Adults (2009)

*Along for the Ride.* New York, NY: Viking, 2009.

**Released:** June 16, 2009

**First Printing:** 250,000 copies

**Summary:** Auden hasn't slept at night for years. It's her way of dealing with her parent's bickering. Now they're divorced, and she's living with her father and his new wife for the summer. Nothing is the same. Is it possible that people can truly change?

**Sales:** The book debuted at number one on the *New York Times* children's chapter books best-seller list. The paperback of *Along for the Ride* was on the *New York Times* children's paperback best-seller list for thirteen weeks.

**Awards and Honors:** ALA Best Books for Young Adults (2010), ALA Teens' Top Ten (2010), ALA Amazing Audiobooks for Young Adults (2010), ALA Popular Paperbacks for Young Adults (2012)

*What Happened to Goodbye.* New York, NY: Viking, 2011.

**Released:** May 10, 2011

**First Printing:** 500,000 copies

**Summary:** Mclean's dad is a restaurant fixer. As soon as she settles into a new school, it's time to move again. The good part is that she can experiment with how she presents herself to people. At least she can until they move one more time and that is suddenly not an option.

**Sales:** *What Happened to Goodbye* hit number two on the *New York Times* children's chapter books best-seller list.

**Awards and Honors:** ALA Best Fiction for Young Adults (2012)

*The Moon and More.* New York, NY: Viking, 2013.

**Released:** June 4, 2013

**First Printing:** 1,000,000 copies

**Summary:** During her last summer before college, Emaline begins a romance with Theo, who is in town working on a movie.

CRITICAL REVIEWS

### *That Summer* (1996)

"Displaying a flair for evocative names and well-timed plot twists, Dessen takes her tall and usually levelheaded teen through two weddings and a succession of disturbing, often comic, surprises, to a climactic explosion. Haven enjoys a nicely articulated love/hate relationship with her sister, ostensibly a superficial cheerleader type who turns out to be wiser than she seems…Seeing everyone else building new lives, Haven starts to think about her own future, too."—*Kirkus Reviews*, August 1, 1996

### *Someone Like You* (1998)

"Dessen deals accurately, sensitively, and smoothly with growing up in suburbia. Halley and Scarlett's friendship resonates with affection and honesty, and the predictable but necessary separation of mothers and daughters is portrayed with tender acuity. Experiences and conversations avoid falling into cliché; all of the characters are fully developed and worth getting to know."—*School Library Journal,* June 1, 1998

### *Keeping the Moon* (1999)

"Rich in sharply observed relationships, deftly inserted wisdom, romances ending and beginning, and characters who are not afraid to pick themselves up and try again, Dessen's tale will leave readers thoughtful, amused, reassured—and sorry when it concludes."—*Kirkus Reviews*, August 15, 1999

"The nifty and not-so-nifty relationships between men and women are observed through the eyes of a teen just on the verge of exploring such things on her own level. The love interests are varied, from a deceitful professional athlete for Morgan to a sincere artist surviving as a short-order cook for Colie. Through it all, readers are shown that 'ya-ya' type friendships are a balm to protect young women while they're kissing toads they thought were princes."—*School Library Journal*, September 1, 1999

***Dreamland* (2000)**

"Her parents, the stereotypically meddling mom and stiff, emotionally distant father…are so caught up in their own concerns, and particularly in Cassandra's disappearance, that they fail to notice the difference in Caitlin (including what seems to be alarming physical evidence), pushing the limits of plausibility. For all these shortcuts, however, the characterizations have an unmistakable depth; readers may grow impatient with Caitlin and the obliviousness of her nearest and dearest, but they will believe she is real."—*Publishers Weekly*, September 4, 2000

"Many young women may not only want to read this story but need to read it as a way to discuss an often overlooked aspect of teenage dating life."—*The Book Report*

**_This Lullaby_ (2002)**

"This modern-day romance narrated by a cynical heroine offers a balance of wickedly funny moments and universal teen traumas. High school graduate Remy has some biting commentary about love...But when rocker Dexter 'crashes' into her life, her resolve to remain unattached starts to crack. Readers will need to hold on to their hats as they accompany Remy on her whirlwind ride, avoiding, circling and finally surrendering to Cupid's arrows. Almost as memorable as her summer romance with a heartwarmingly flawed suitor is the cast of idiosyncratic characters who watch from the sidelines."—*Publishers Weekly*, May 2002

"As Dessen's body of work expands, her novels deepen. With its deceptively simple summer romance plot, this book documents adolescent life with perception and acuity. Remy, her family, and friends are unique and fully realized characters with complementing story lines. Not one for typecasting, Dessen creates characters with unapologetic faults and no moralizing... With Dessen's sympathy, accuracy, and genuine respect for her characters and readers, this novel is sure to become another favorite of high school readers."—*VOYA Reviews*, 2002

### *The Truth About Forever* (2004)

"All of Dessen's characters, from Macy, who narrates to the bone, to Kristy, whose every word has life and attitude, to Monica, who says almost nothing but oozes nuance, are fully and beautifully drawn. Their dialogue is natural and believable, and their care for one another is palpable. The prose is fueled with humor...and as many good comedians do, Dessen uses it to throw light onto darker subjects."—*School Library Journal,* June 1, 2004

"After her father's death, runner Macy Queen tries to conform to the expectations of her distant mother and perfectionist boyfriend. A summer catering job introduces Macy to some well-drawn peripheral characters, while providing the impetus for self-exploration and eventual communication with her family. This meandering tale explores different approaches to grief but is marred by a predictable ending."—*Horn Book Magazine*, October 1, 2004

***Just Listen*** **(2006)**

"A cut above chick lit, Dessen's tale of an 'It' girl who only seems to have it all has sharply drawn characters, serious themes (anorexia, rape), and a page-turner of a plot. Aimed at high schoolers, it has Mom appeal, too."—*People Magazine*, May 29, 2006

"In delicate, unassuming prose, naturally flowing dialogue, and a complex, credible plot, Dessen portrays Annabel's socially endorsed self-repression with depth and intensity. The romance with Owen, which forms the core of the story, is everything a romance should be—challenging, heartfelt, and most of all organic. In the end, families are healed, friendships are resurrected, and love—in all its unexpected incarnations—triumphs."—*Horn Book Magazine*, May 1, 2006

***Lock and Key*** **(2008)**

"After her mother leaves, seventeen-year-old Ruby is placed in the care of her sister. Ruby strikes up a tentative friendship with Nate, whose father is abusive. The intricacy of relationships shines in this in-depth exploration of family, trust, and responsibility. The complex, deeply sympathetic characters are pure pleasure to spend time with."—*Horn Book Magazine*, October 1, 2008

### *Along for the Ride* (2009)

"Even Dessen's minor characters are multifaceted and interesting. Readers will be most absorbed by Auden and Eli's romantic friendship, the type soul mates are born of, played out in the bike shop, Colby's all-night laundromat, and coffee shops. This summer vacation-themed story will be savored."—*School Library Journal*, June 1, 2009

"Taut, witty first-person narration allows readers to both identify with Auden's insecurities and recognize her unfair, acerbic criticisms of people. It's Eli, a fellow insomniac, with whom she connects, and together they tick off items on her kid to-do list (food fights, bowling, paper-delivery route) while the rest of the town sleeps. The spark between these two sad teens and the joyful examples of girl connectivity deepen this ostensibly lighthearted, summer-fun story."—*Kirkus Reviews*, May 15, 2009

### *What Happened to Goodbye* (2011)

"Readers can count on Dessen; she's a pro at creating characters caught at a nexus of change, who have broken relationships and who need to make decisions...Even though Mclean's path is clear from the get-go, readers will enjoy every minute they spend with her."—*Kirkus Reviews*, April 15, 2011

"These characters are real and interesting and the story line unrolls smoothly and with purpose. There's a slight lack of tension, however, that keeps it from being truly compelling. Still, Dessen's fans will be happy to devour this latest offering and will surely be able to relate to one of several engaging and evolving teenagers that populate the novel."—*School Library Journal*, June 2011

# TIMELINE

**1970** Sarah Dessen is born on June 6 in Evanston, Illinois.

**1973** Dessen's parents take jobs at the University of North Carolina and the family moves to Chapel Hill.

**1988** Dessen graduates from Chapel Hill High School.

**1993** Dessen graduates from the University of North Carolina at Chapel Hill with a Bachelor of Arts in English, with highest honors in creative writing.

**1996** Dessen's first novel, *That Summer*, is released.

**c. 1997** Dessen is offered a job as a lecturer in the creative writing department at UNC. She stops waitressing.

**1998** *Someone Like You*, Dessen's second novel and her first published by Viking, is released.

**1999** *Keeping the Moon* is released in September.

**2000** *Dreamland* is released. Dessen marries Jay Earl Marks on June 10.

**2002** *This Lullaby* is released in May.

**2003** *How to Deal*, a motion picture based on *That Summer* and *Someone Like You*, is released.

**2004** *The Truth About Forever* is released in May.

**2006** *Just Listen* is released. The book spends eighteen weeks on the *New York Times* children's chapter book best-seller list.

**2007** Dessen's daughter, Sasha Clementine, is born on September 2.

**2008** *Lock and Key* is released. The hardcover of *Lock and Key* and the paperback edition of *Just Listen* spend a combined thirty-one weeks on the *New York Times* best-seller list.

**2009** *Along for the Ride* is released. It debuts at number one on the *New York Times* children's chapter books list. Penguin Young Readers launches Sarahland, a social networking community that has attracted thousands of members.

**2011** Dessen's tenth book, *What Happened to Goodbye*, is published. It debuts at number two on the *New York Times* children's chapter book best-seller list.

**2013** *The Moon and More* is published with an initial print run of one million copies.

# GLOSSARY

**AMPLE** More than enough to satisfy a need.

**ANGST** A feeling of anxiety or insecurity.

**ASPIRE** To seek to achieve a certain goal.

**CHARACTERIZATION** The creation of effective characters.

**CLASSICIST** A scholar of the literature of the ancient Greeks and Romans.

**COMPELLING** Able to capture and hold a person's attention.

**DUBIOUS** Of questionable value or quality; untrustworthy.

**EMBELLISH** To make more interesting or entertaining by adding details, especially fictitious ones.

**ESCHEW** To stay clear of; avoid.

**FAÇADE** A false or misleading front.

**FERVOR** Intense excitement and enthusiasm.

**GRAVITATE** To move toward or be attracted to something.

**HONE** To sharpen or make more effective.

**INSPIRATION** Something that stimulates a person to creative thought or action.

**INTEGRAL** Necessary for completeness; essential.

**LITERARY AGENT** A professional who represents an author to publishers.

**METHODICAL** Done according to a careful and organized procedure.

**NOVELIST** A person who writes novels.

**NURTURE** To help grow or develop.

**PROXIMITY** Nearness in space or time.

**QUASH** To put an end to; extinguish.

**RESONATE** To be understood on an emotional level; to strike a chord.

**SELF-DEPRECATING** Having a tendency to belittle oneself or focus on one's own shortcomings.

**SENIOR THESIS** A large project involving original research or scholarship that some students complete in the senior year of college to fulfill a graduation requirement.

**TENACITY** The ability to stick with something when difficult.

**TUMULTUOUS** Marked by turbulence, disorder, or upheaval.

**VOICE** The personality of a piece of writing.

**WRITER'S BLOCK** An inability to proceed with a piece of writing.

**YOUNG ADULT (YA)** A category of books intended for readers in their teens, often dealing with issues of concern to them.

American Society of Journalists and Authors (ASJA)
1501 Broadway, Suite 403
New York, NY 10036
(212) 997-0947
Web site: http://www.asja.org
The American Society of Journalists and Authors is the nation's professional organization of independent nonfiction writers.

Canadian Authors Association (CAA)
74 Mississaga Street East
Orillia, ON L3V 1V5
Canada
(705) 653-0323
Web site: http://www.canauthors.org
The Canadian Authors Association is dedicated to writers helping writers at the local level.

Canadian Writers Society (CWA)
c/o 9770, Boulevard Saint-Laurent
Montreal, QC H3L 2N3
Canada
(514) 707-9396
Web site: http://www.canadianwriterssociety.com
The Canadian Writers Society is a group of writers who share their work and ideas.

Highlights Foundation
814 Court Street
Honesdale, PA 18431

(570) 253-1192
Web site: http://www.highlightsfoundation.org
The Highlights Foundation is dedicated to improving the quality of children's literature by helping authors and illustrators hone their craft.

International Reading Association (IRA)
444 North Capitol Street NW, Suite 640
Washington, DC 20001
(202) 624-8800
Web site: http://www.reading.org/resources/booklists/youngadultschoices.aspx
This nonprofit, global network of individuals and institutions is committed to worldwide literacy. Its Young Adults' Choices project develops an annual list of new books selected by teen readers in order to encourage adolescents to read.

Library of Congress
101 Independence Avenue SE
Washington, DC 20540
(202) 707-5000
Web site: http://www.loc.gov/bookfest
The Library of Congress is the largest library in the world. In addition to offering resources for families, children, and teens, it hosts the Library of Congress National Book Festival each year. Held in September, it is two days of writers, poets, and pavilions on the National Mall in Washington, D.C.

Penguin Group (USA)
375 Hudson Street
New York, NY 10014
(212) 366-2000
Web site: http://www.us.penguingroup.com
Penguin Group (USA) is a leading U.S. adult and children's trade book publisher. It publishes under a wide range of imprints and trademarks, among them Viking, which is home to Sarah Dessen's books. Readers can learn more about Dessen and her work on the company's Web site.

Romance Writers of America (RWA)
14615 Benfer Road
Houston, TX 77069
(832) 717-5200
Web site: http://www.rwa.org
Romance Writers of America is dedicated to advancing the professional interests of career-focused romance writers.

Society of Children's Book Writers and Illustrators (SCBWI)
8271 Beverly Boulevard
Los Angeles, CA 90048
(323) 728-1010
Web site: http://www.scbwi.org
The Society of Children's Book Writers and Illustrators is the largest existing organization for writers and illustrators.

Young Adult Library Services Association (YALSA)
50 East Huron Street
Chicago, IL 60611-2795
(800) 545-2433
Web site: http://www.ala.org/yalsa
A division of the American Library Association (ALA), YALSA is a national association of library professionals working to expand and strengthen library services for teens. It builds the capacity of libraries and librarians to engage, serve, and empower teen readers.

## WEB SITES

Due to the changing nature of Internet links, Rosen Publishing has developed an online list of Web sites related to the subject of this book. This site is updated regularly. Please use this link to access the list:

http://www.rosenlinks.com/AAA/dessen

# FOR FURTHER READING

Ackerman, Angela, and Becca Puglisi. *The Emotion Thesaurus: A Writer's Guide to Character Expression*. Lexington, KY: The Authors, 2012.

Anderson, Laurie Halse. *Wintergirls*. New York, NY: Viking, 2009.

Benke, Karen. *Rip the Page! Adventures in Creative Writing*. Boston, MA: Trumpeter, 2010.

Bodden, Valerie. *Creating the Character: Dialogue and Characterization*. Mankato, MN: Creative Education, 2009.

Brewer, Robert Lee. *2013 Writer's Market*. Cincinnati, OH: Writer's Digest Books, 2012.

Burroway, Janet. *Imaginative Writing: The Elements of Craft*. Harlow, England: Longman, 2010.

Burroway, Janet, Elizabeth Stuckey-French, and Ned Stuckey-French. *Writing Fiction: A Guide to Narrative Craft*. Upper Saddle River, NJ: Pearson Education, 2010.

Cameron, Julia. *The Creative Life: True Tales of Inspiration*. New York, NY: Jeremy P. Tarcher/ Penguin, 2010.

Casagrande, June. *It Was the Best of Sentences, It Was the Worst of Sentences: A Writer's Guide to Crafting Killer Sentences*. Berkeley, CA: Ten Speed Press, 2010.

Clark, Roy Peter. *Writing Tools: 50 Essential Strategies for Every Writer*. New York, NY: Little, Brown and Company, 2008.

Colasanti, Susane. *Something Like Fate*. New York, NY: Viking, 2010.

Corbett, David. *The Art of Character: Creating Memorable Characters for Fiction, Film, and TV*. New York, NY: Penguin Books, 2013.

Ellis, Sherry, and Laurie Lamson. *Now Write! Screenwriting: Exercises by Today's Best Writers and Teachers*. New York, NY: Jeremy P. Tarcher/ Penguin, 2010.

Fogarty, Mignon. *Grammar Girl's Quick and Dirty Tips for Better Writing*. New York, NY: Henry Holt and Co., 2008.

Fogarty, Mignon, and Erwin Haya. *Grammar Girl Presents the Ultimate Writing Guide for Students*. New York, NY: Henry Holt and Co., 2011.

Forman, Gayle. *If I Stay: A Novel.* New York, NY: Dutton Books, 2009.

Glenn, Wendy J. *Sarah Dessen: From Burritos to Box Office*. Lanham, MD: Scarecrow Press, 2005.

Griffin, Paul. *Stay with Me.* New York, NY: Dial Books, 2011.

Hahn, Daniel, Leonie Flynn, and Susan Reuben. *The Ultimate Teen Book Guide*. New York, NY: Walker & Co., 2008.

Hale, Constance. *Vex, Hex, Smash, Smooch: Let Verbs Power Your Writing*. New York, NY: W. W. Norton & Co., 2012.

Han, Jenny. *The Summer I Turned Pretty.* New York, NY: Simon & Schuster Books for Young Readers, 2009.

Kress, Nancy. *Beginnings, Middles and Ends*. Cincinnati, OH: Writer's Digest Books, 2011.

Maass, Donald. *Writing 21st Century Fiction: High-Impact Techniques for Exceptional Storytelling*. Cincinnati, OH: Writer's Digest Books, 2012.

Nelson, Jandy. *The Sky Is Everywhere*. New York, NY: Dial Books, 2010.

Ray, Robert J., and Robert J. Ray. *The Weekend Novelist Rewrites the Novel: A Step-by-Step Guide to Perfecting Your Work*. New York, NY: Watson-Guptill Publications, 2010.

Smith, Jennifer E. *The Statistical Probability of Love at First Sight*. New York, NY: Little, Brown, 2012.

# BIBLIOGRAPHY

Azzam, Julie. "Preview: Sarah Dessen Tells the Truth About High School." *Pittsburgh Post-Gazette*, January 16, 2013. Retrieved January 18, 2013 (http://www.post-gazette.com/stories/ae/books/preview-sarah-dessen-tells-the-truth-about-high-school-670517).

Corbett, Sue. "Children's Bookshelf Talks with Sarah Dessen." PublishersWeekly.com, March 9, 2006. Retrieved January 5, 2013 (http://www.publishersweekly.com/pw/by-topic/authors/interviews/article/9878-children-s-bookshelf-talks-with-sarah-dessen.html).

Dessen, Sarah. "Bio/Press Kit." SarahDessen.com. Retrieved January 8, 2013 (http://www.sarahdessen.com/press-kit).

Dessen, Sarah. "Dreamland." SarahDessen.com. Retrieved January 5, 2013 (http://www.sarahdessen.com/book/dreamland).

Dessen, Sarah. "The Friday Five!" SarahDessen.com, April 27, 2012. Retrieved January 3, 2013 (http://sarahdessen.com/3038/blog/the-friday-five-53).

Dessen, Sarah. "The Friday Five!" SarahDessen.com, July 13, 2012. Retrieved January 3, 2013 (http://sarahdessen.com/3192/blog/the-friday-five-62).

Dessen, Sarah. "The Friday Five!" SarahDessen.com, August 10, 2012. Retrieved January 3,

2013 (http://sarahdessen.com/3251/the-five/the-friday-five-65).

Dessen, Sarah. "The Friday Five!" SarahDessen.com, January 18, 2013. Retrieved January 8, 2013 (http://sarahdessen.com/3483/blog/the-friday-five-83).

Dessen, Sarah. "Just Listen." SarahDessen.com. Retrieved January 5, 2013 (http://www.sarahdessen.com/book/just-listen).

Dessen, Sarah. "Keeping the Moon." SarahDessen.com. Retrieved January 8, 2013 (http://www.sarahdessen.com/book/keeping-the-moon).

Dessen, Sarah. "Lock and Key." SarahDessen.com. Retrieved January 5, 2013 (http://www.sarahdessen.com/book/lock-and-key).

Dessen, Sarah. "Long Time…" SarahDessen.com, July 27, 2011. Retrieved January 8, 2013 (http://sarahdessen.com/2634/blog/long-time).

Dessen, Sarah. "Someone Like You." SarahDessen.com. Retrieved January 3, 2013 (http://www.sarahdessen.com/book/someone-like-you).

Dessen, Sarah. "Sunday…" SarahDessen.com, January 15, 2012. Retrieved January 5, 2013 (http://sarahdessen.com/2932/blog/sunday-2).

Dessen, Sarah. "That Summer." SarahDessen.com. Retrieved January 3, 2013 (http://sarahdessen.com/book/that-summer).

Dessen, Sarah. "This Lullaby." SarahDessen.com. Retrieved January 5, 2013 (http://www.sarahdessen.com/book/this-lullaby).

Dessen, Sarah. "The Truth About Forever." SarahDessen.com. Retrieved January 5, 2013 (http://www.sarahdessen.com/book/the-truth-about-forever).

Devereaux, Elizabeth. "Someone Like You." NYTimes.com, September 20, 1998. Retrieved January 5, 2013 (http://www.nytimes.com/books/98/09/20/reviews/980920.rv104457.html).

IMDb.com. "How to Deal." 2003. Retrieved January 5, 2013 (http://www.imdb.com/title/tt0319524).

IMDb.com. "Reviews and Ratings for *How to Deal*." Retrieved January 4, 2013 (http://www.imdb.com/title/tt0319524/reviews).

Keane, Shannon Rigney. "Sarah Dessen: Writing the Real Girl." Girls Leadership Institute, March 26, 2010. Retrieved March 5, 2013 (http://www.girlsleadershipinstitute.org/blog/2010/03/26/sarah-dessen-writing-real-girl).

Kirkus.com. "*Along for the Ride* by Sarah Dessen." May 20, 2010. Retrieved January 3, 2013 (http://www.kirkusreviews.com/book-reviews/sarah-dessen/along-for-the-ride).

Kirkus.com. "*What Happened to Goodbye* by Sarah Dessen." April 5, 2011. Retrieved January 5, 2013 (http://www.kirkusreviews.com/book-reviews/sarah-dessen/what-happened-goodbye).

Maughan, Shannon. "Hitching a 'Ride' with Sarah Dessen." PublishersWeekly.com, May 21, 2009. Retrieved January 5, 2013 (http://www.publishersweekly.com/pw/by-topic/childrens/childrens-book-news/article/4161-hitching-a-ride-with-sarah-dessen.html).

NPR.org. "Your Favorites: 100 Best-Ever Teen Novels." August 7, 2012. Retrieved March 5, 2013 (http://www.npr.org/2012/08/07/157795366/your-favorites-100-best-ever-teen-novels).

Penguin Young Readers. "Get to Know Sarah Dessen: Part II." YouTube.com, March 1, 2011. Retrieved January 5, 2013 (http://www.youtube.com/watch?v=tT9H5etQiro&feature=youtu.be).

Penguin Young Readers. "Sarah Dessen Talks About Her New Book *What Happened to Goodbye*." YouTube.com, March 15, 2011. Retrieved January 3, 2013 (http://www.youtube.com/watch?v=gkzOIC-Uifl&feature=youtu.be).

RottenTomatoes.com. "How to Deal." 2003. Retrieved January 5, 2013 (http://www.rottentomatoes.com/m/how_to_deal).

Sutton, Roger. "An Interview with Sarah Dessen." *Horn Book Magazine*, May/June 2009. Retrieved March 10, 2013 (http://archive

.hbook.com/magazine/articles/2009/may09_dessen.asp).

wordsmithkari. "My Top 5 Experiences with Authors." *An Adventure a Day*, March 20, 2013. Retrieved March 29, 2013 (http://wordsmithkari.wordpress.com/2013/03/20/my-top-5-experiences-with-authors).

YA Bibliophile. "The World of Sarah Dessen." May 10, 2011. Retrieved March 5, 2013 (http://www.yabibliophile.com/2011/05/world-of-sarah-dessen.html).

# INDEX


## A

abandonment, as theme, 49–51
*Along for the Ride*, 32, 48, 49, 51, 55, 60, 61, 63, 64, 68, 69
Annabel (character), 61
*Are You There, God? It's Me, Margaret*, 14
Auden (character), 51–53, 55, 61, 63, 68

## B

Barnz, Daniel, 27
basketball, 15, 32
*Beastly*, 27
Beber, Neena, 42
Betts, Doris, 20
Blume, Judy, 14

## C

Caitlin (character), 54
Colby (setting), 32, 71
Colie (character), 64–65
Collins, Suzanne, 26

## D

*Daisy Chain, The*, 20
dating violence, as theme, 54
Dessen, Alan, 10, 11, 13
Dessen, Cynthia, 10, 11, 13
Dessen, Michael, 33–34
Dessen, Sarah
  childhood, 9–13
  in college, 19–21
  and communication with readers, 70–71, 73, 74
  in high school, 13–17
  marriage and children, 20, 66–71
  sources of inspiration, 29–34
divorce, as theme, 51–54
*Dreamland*, 54, 55, 64

## E

Eli (character), 60
Emaline (character), 71

## F

*Fault in Our Stars, The*, 26
Feldman, Leigh, 28
Flying Burrito restaurant, 20, 22, 32
"Friday Five!, The," 70
friendship, as theme, 55–57

G

Green, John, 20
grieving, as theme, 57–60

H

Halley (character), 41, 42, 44, 55, 60
Haven (character), 25–28, 39, 40
high school angst, as theme, 61
Holden, Alexandra, 42
*How to Deal*, 35, 42–46
*Hunger Games, The*, 26

J

Jordan, Michael, 15
*Just Listen*, 48, 61

K

*Keeping the Moon*, 64
Kilner, Claire, 42

L

Lakeview (setting), 37, 46
*Lock and Key*, 49, 68
*Looking for Alaska*, 26
Lowry, Lois, 14

M

Macon (character), 41, 44
Macy (character), 57–60
Marks, Jay Earl, 20, 40, 66, 70
Mclean (character), 53, 55–57, 64
Meyer, Stephenie, 26
*Moon and More, The*, 71, 75
Moore, Mandy, 42

P

*Pretty Little Liars*, 27

R

relationships, as theme, 61–64
Remy (character), 63
Rogerson (character), 54
Rowling, J. K., 26
Ruby (character), 49–50

S

Sarah-land, 74, 75
Scarlett (character), 41, 42, 44, 55, 60, 61

self-esteem, as theme, 64–65
Shepard, Sara, 27
*Someone Like You*, 35, 39–41, 42, 46–47, 55, 60, 61
*Summer to Die, A*, 14
Sumner (character), 40

T

*That Summer*, 20, 23–25, 29, 35, 37–39, 40, 41, 42, 64
*This Lullaby*, 48, 63
*Truth About Forever, The*, 48, 57
*Twilight*, 26, 61

W

*What Happened to Goodbye*, 32, 53, 55, 71, 75
writer's block, 30

## ABOUT THE AUTHOR

Gina Hagler is an award-winning author who writes on a variety of topics. Her work has appeared in several periodicals for teens. The writing program she created for elementary and middle school students is now in three schools in Montgomery County, Maryland. A member of the Society of Children's Book Writers and Illustrators, she is completing *SciGirls*, her first young adult novel.

## PHOTO CREDITS

Cover, pp. 3, 6–7, 24–25, 31, 78 KPO Photo; pp. 10–11 Barry Winiker/Photolibrary/Getty Images; p. 12 Chezlov /Shutterstock.com; pp. 16–17 Grant Halverson/Getty Images; pp. 18–19 Michael Ochs Archives/Getty Images; p. 23, 36–37 iStockphoto/Thinkstock; p. 27 Alberto E. Rodriguez/Getty Images; pp. 32–33 CBS Photo Archive /Getty Images; pp. 38–39 Piotr Marcinski/Shutterstock .com; pp. 42–43 © Courtesy of New Line Cinema /Entertainment Pictures/ZUMA Press; pp. 44–45 © AP Images; pp. 50–51 Andrzej Wilusz/Shutterstock.com; pp. 52–53 Colin Hawkins/Cultura/Getty Images; pp. 56–57 Pixland/Thinkstock; pp. 58–59 Diego Cervo/Shutterstock .com; pp. 62–63 Maria Teijeiro/Photodisc/Thinkstock; p. 67 Biddiboo/Stone/Getty Images; pp. 72–73 Courtesy of Ronni Davis Selzer; pp. 76–77 Yuri Arcurs/Shutterstock .com; cover and interior pages background (marbleized texture) javarman/Shutterstock.com; cover and interior pages (book) www.iStockphoto.com/Andrzej Tokarski; interior pages background (landscape) Steve Schwettman /Shutterstock.com.

Designer: Nicole Russo; Editor: Andrea Sclarow Paskoff; Photo Researcher: Karen Huang